TAKING THE H̶̶̶̶̶̶̶̶̶̶̶̶ ̶̶̶̶̶̶̶̶̶̶̶̶CENSUS

alexis ivy

saturnalia books

Distributed by Independent Publishers Group Chicago

TAKING THE HOMELESS CENSUS

alexis ivy

Saturnalia Books
105 Woodside Rd.
Ardmore, PA 19003
info@saturnaliabooks.com

ISBN: 978-1-947817-14-2 (print), 978-1-947817-15-9 (ebook)
Library of Congress Control Number: 2019952592

Cover and book design by Robin Vuchnich

Distributed by:
Independent Publishing Group
814 N. Franklin St.
Chicago, IL 60610
800-888-4741

Grateful acknowledgement is made to the following journals in which these poems, first appeared, sometimes in different versions:

Atlanta Review: "The Poem as Metaphor"
Borderlands: Texas Poetry Review: "The Poem Sitting on a Crate"
Boston Literary Magazine: "Billiards"
Common Ground Review: "Having a Second Cup"
Eclipse: "Dream on the 17th Floor"
EDGE: "The Pin-Up Girl I Want to Be"
Exit 7: "Home" and "The Poem Showed Up at My Door"
Free State Review: "I Tell the Janitor I'm Moving Out" and "The Poem in Public"
Heartland Review: "The A-Street Shelter: i", "The A-Street Shelter: xi"
J Journal: "The A-Street Shelter: xii"
Lake Effect: "Goodnight is Never Goodnight"

Lalitamba: "Taking the Homeless Census" and "The A-Street Shelter: *x*"
Merrimack Review: "Spare Change"
New Plains Review: "Elegy"
NOUS: "The A-Street Shelter: *viii*"
One Person's Trash: "The Poem, An Ars Poetica", "The A-Street Shelter: *ii*"
Pittsburgh Poetry Review: "I've Eaten Spicy"
Poesy: "My Mother's Advice"
Poetry East: "The A-Street Shelter: *xiv*"
San Pedro River Review: "Playing Cribbage with My Father"
Saranac Review: "The A-Street Shelter: *v*", "The A-Street Shelter: *xiii*",
"Night is All I've Had of France"
Spare Change News: "Reading about Death Row in *The Times*" "Day Shift at Rosie's Place"
Spillway: "The A-Street Shelter: *ix*"
Tusculum Review: "Missing the Poem in Europe"
Worcester Review: "The Poem at the Swings"

"Map of Boston, 2013" appeared in *Voices from the Porch: Poems, Essays and Fiction from Favorite Gathering Spaces*, edited by Maureen A. Sherbondy, Main Street Rag, 2013.

"Map of Boston, 2013" was a winner of the *Prose and Poetry Program* at Boston City Hall, judged by Poet Laureate Sam Cornish, 2014.

"Home" was part of *Poetry on the T Program* sponsored by Mass Poetry, January 2017.

"Woman Stopped at Customs" first appeared in *Not My President Anthology*, edited by Thoughtcrime Press, 2017.

"The A-Street Shelter: *x*" was a winner of the Prose and Poetry Program at Boston City Hall, judged by Poet Laureate Porsha Olayiwola, 2019.

Thank you to Barbara Helfgott Hyett and the PoemWorks community for making these poems heartbreaking. Thank you to the Massachusetts Cultural Council for granting me the Fellowship in Poetry in 2018 and for believing in my work.

In tribute to
The People of Albany Street Shelter

Contents

I.

...we are each other's
harvest:
we are each other's
business:
we are each other's
magnitude and bond.

—Gwendolyn Brooks

The A-Street Shelter: A Crown of Sonnets

i

Past their home, I came to poetry,
their home where I shout *Female on the floor*
whenever I enter, I have come to see
who's turned blue, turned dead, where there's a fight
to de-escalate. If someone's feet
stink, there'll be blood, and I don't want
to circle "guest assault", write out neat
and tidy *Restriction* with my name. Taunted
Troublemaker gets high, Medicine-Taker
breathes unevenly in bed ten, the leaden
light stays on, bed no one wants. Tyler,
shit-kicked for the way he snores. New beds
given each day, *Pick a chip from the tin.*
No one's at home here: No one's in.

ii

No one's at home here: No one's in.
The cook thinks, *they can only get one plate*, it's
the drunks who try for two, bread stuffed in
their pockets *'cause she starves us*. Dinner is
served early-bird with outbursts: *that was my
seat*, everyone pushing to the front of the line,
one man's face pressed into the greens and fried
mashed potatoes she's undercooked.   For lunch,
donated sandwiches. She'll wait a day so
she can serve them stale.   One table of men
are given okra and corn, pie. She'll slice a whole
smiling melon into six pieces for them.
Their afros, cut the same: so statuesque
as clean as their cocaine. They deal the best.

iii

As clean as their cocaine. They deal the best
on the first of the month— street queen Gail buys
it all for her pimp with her SSI check,
smiles until the last hit then her eyes
are hungry again. And here comes Pete
robbed a market when he opens up
his backpack, drunk on Vodka, he sleeps
it off in a chair. The girl they call *Trollop*
signed up for Disability. I knew
her bloating was from Hep C. She leaves
the mice her bread crumbs, *it's their home too*.
Mice in the male room, mice in the beef's grease.
So much for free when you are living in
the shelter. Paying for every minute of it.

iv

The shelter paying for every minute of it:
The first to die on my shift, the Vietnam
Vet. Was he someone I could have saved? In
my last round I glance at each bed, watched Tom's
blankets go up and down, *sleep* I thought.
I had lifted his weightless arms. Did
that kill him? It was me who made his cot.
Me, who scanned him in, me who found his
stash of whiskey down in the leather seat
of his wheelchair— seat trenched in war.
I dump the booze in the nurse's excrete
drain. Pee was the reason he was bed four.
Piss bed. Dead bed. His bed. On this last round
I wear latex gloves, lay him down to rest.

v

I wear latex gloves, lay it down to rest—
the bag I had him empty on the check-
in desk to search for drugs in his mess.
Something's hidden there. I should've instead
made him take it out. But I stuck my glove
into and a needle pricked me. I held
my breath to look. Squeezed to see if my thumb
would bleed. It didn't. Was that needle used? Tell
him his rubber tie that made his purple
veins brighten must be discarded. Part of his gear.
I know puss, know when an infection bubbles
up red, swell red, rot red. And I know where
the neck vein bruises. Know the marks on the hand.
Arm used up, those marks he couldn't hide.

vi

Arm used up, marks he couldn't hide
I'm forced to be the angel Gabriel.
Checked under the carwash awning for him, I
check the redemption center, his hustle—
cans. Listened for his supermarket carriage,
cans full and chattering as he wheeled it.
I found him, carried him a message.
I was a sworn saint, here for my eight-
hour shift to find undocumented Jose.
The hospital called, and he needs to go
asap or else they'll have Jose's
arm cut off. Gangrene. They'll sew
and redress his wound. Fluent enough to plead—
es una emergencia! He knew his needs.

vii

Es una emergencia! She knew. I need
her to know, *You can stay one night every ninety
nights.* I had to tell her. Tell her she
has had her one night. I had to deny
her. Suffer that. Then her fist came down on
the side of my head right above my ear,
hit my skull, and she pounded down on
me like a stuck ceiling fan, thrash of gears
and I froze. Just plain stood there as she hit
me. I didn't feel the hurt, didn't split my lip, didn't
pull my hair, or tangle up strands, didn't spit
on me like my brother did. The rest of my shift
I stayed. If I left, I'd leave feeling exiled.
I had to take it when I was a child.

viii
I had to take it when I was a child—
Pam said— and I nod a yes, I am
like her, show up for her, promise I'll
be there for all the homeless I can,
stow blankets, hand out donated quilts.
Give people sleeping out in the rain ponchos,
feed them protein bars, ham and cheese melts
I make before my shift. Nuts I chose
for Vegan Joe. He likes to be known. And I
see *her*, Pam, drunk, can't leave the ground where
she sprawls. Because today she's sick of life.
I tell her the world I know with a walk-
in center for women. My job sweaters me.
I'm careful. Refuse to bleed, used to bleed.

ix

I'm careful. Refuse to bleed, used to bleed.
I first see Sharon at the end of her
intake, drunk. She isn't wearing her teeth
like she was last week when we were
hugging hello at a NA meeting,
share with our group the truth about ourselves.
She knows my deep darks. Can't have her living
here, this is the one place no one can tell
on me. This was my safe place. Place for me
not to have my history. Maybe she'll leave.
Maybe she'll want to clean up. Maybe
she'll go to a program, get sober, have teeth
again. Maybe I'll give her my business—
I've got your number, she says, *Alexis.*

x

I've got your number, she says, *Alexis*,
I wasn't there when she took off. It was
the morning shift and she must be in bliss
in her new one-bedroom, all the walls were
pine, she would put up her heirloom
curtains. Her kitchen drawers, she's filled
with silverware stolen from the lunch room.
She died doped up, so high, her needle still
in her vein. Kept wishing she were
here. I would have Narcan-ed her not breathing.
She was found on her so-new mattress, wrapped
in her curtains, hadn't gotten bedding
yet— *Housing*—she finally had it—a headstone.
In the God sense of things, a place of her own.

xi

In a God sense of things, a place of his own,
a man asleep on the bedrock construction
site. It's ten below. He must sting, his moan
mildewed with booze, he wants nothing from
me. I didn't want to leave him but I did.
I wish he'd wanted a place to go. Outside
is where I work—and out here people die:
One kid shot— stole pills off the wrong guy,
chicken-choked, heart fails, drunk-falls-down stairs.
Tonight I save no one. I wish I'd given
him mittens, handwarmers, gloves to wear
I wanted to make the run, would have driven
him to shelter so he'd be warmed, yes,
would've cleaned the back seat of his sickness.

xii

Would've clean the backseat of his sickness
just so I could know the eye of one-eyed
Sid, his eye, torn shut like that, tearless,
how it got to be that way— and why
it took so long for his left lid to wake,
crusted shut each morning, his caged eye.
He asks for socks. I ask him, *snowflake
or unpatterned—Warm*, he says. A necktie
I get him. His court date is the ninth. *No
thanks*, he says to a face saving button-
down shirt from the clothing closet. Won't
take a razor to shave. Flirts, subtle grin,
puts his hand on mine, *you have moonstones,
the two nicest eyes I have ever known.*

xiii

The two nicest eyes I have ever known
sit on a bench. With Kit. I give them
water. *It's beer three so far, chaperone,*
two-eyes tell. Do they pretend that they
ration their beers to please my worry? Kit's
moved on from liquor to Listerine,
her coat is covered in dried bird shit—
I've seen her beg, seen her cop drugs, seen
her talk un-slurred, neatly dressed looking
housed. The cops called us with a Code One Ten—
homeless drunk. Not a crime. Not an anything.
They had just ran out of beer. I can
recognize those fleeing detox cries. See
their out-of-money eyes look to me.

xiv

Their out-of-money eyes look to me
in the train station. I offer to walk
Jane to the shelter. *I'm living at Lori's
house.* It looks like she's been here, parked
on the floor. Hasn't come to the shelter
since her boyfriend died there. ODed. Couldn't
get to his heart, medics cut off his shirt.
I was there. Another night I took
work home with me. I can tell she's high,
a pile of Kit Kat wrappers shine beside
her. Her skull cap is her pillow, the hat
she won't remove. I've been high, outside
waiting for a *him*, I know that story.
Past their home I came to poetry.

No one's at home here: No one's in.
As clean as their cocaine. They deal the best,
the shelter's paying. For every minute of it:
I wear latex gloves, lay them down to rest—
Arm used up, marks they couldn't hide
Es una emergencia! I know their needs,
I had to take it when I was a child.
I'm careful. Refuse to bleed, used to bleed.
I've got your number. They say, *Alexis*,
in the God sense of things. A place of their own
would clean the back seat of our sickness.
The two nicest eyes they have ever known,
their out-of-money eyes look to me.
Past their home, I came to poetry.

I.

As for Me

I like the bus, its particular
iridescence. I like the potholes that make me
hold tight the pole. I want to touch

a stranger's touch, the stranger who
made that pole warm. Give me cracked
vinyl seats, unwiped walls giving up

to the spreadsheet routes,
even the commuter rail to Rockport—
the seaside stops, the boxy cities,

platforms with their un-pushy
No Smoking signs. Fast-faster,
loud-louder and I'm all in

with junkyard bicycle-factory dust,
the good graffiti, and bad graffiti—
the basic color of the world.

You Don't Know a Man,

my father says, *until you've seen his place.*
His first live-alone a triple decker.
Dishes piled up in the sink.
Before is the place my father goes too often.
Only listens to music recorded *before* 1977.
He's dust jackets, vinyl vintage albums—
when I wasn't even in the picture
or the liner notes or the artist's statement.

My mother future-tenses everything.
She's full of desire, the want-of-what-will.
Say we're on vacation on the Cape,
she wants *next year on the Cape.*
Asks for the dessert menu in the middle
of the main course. She worries what'll
happen to me, worries while watching channel 7
waiting for the news of tomorrow's weather.

I smoke a cigarette on purpose right before
I walk into their house so I'll be practically
unhuggable. And there's that photograph of us
on the Cape. Mother, father, brother, their
sunglasses facing into the lens and me,
alone like an orchid. I suffer the unspoken.
When coyotes all get together, they yip.
I want to be part of that howling. Be licked clean.

My Mother's Advice

...prepare a face to meet the faces that you meet
—T.S. Eliot

My mother said to focus on how I look,
not how I feel. If that's what she wants—fine.
I'll be a clown. All-day-all-night laughter
and laugh-a-lot, lost in cars too small

in my too-big shoes—
no room for how I feel. I'll hide my skin
in greasepaint. Do you know how hard it is
to take off greasepaint? How many more

scarves can I pull out of a hat? The further I fly,
shot from a cannon, the more the applause.
I've seen my mother be the show:
It was a full-bottle break of cider vinegar—

kitchen floor, cursed, the stools
ridden with glass, the wallpaper
forest dwarfed. My mother cried
as if the mop and bucket wouldn't do.

Day Shift at Rosie's Place

I have set every table, I peel and cut
one hundred and sixty carrots
for soup, fill every shaker with salt.
Plate Wednesday's Tuna Casserole.
Open canned peaches for when
the oranges run out.
Fold all the aprons, do dishwasher
duty. Set the tables again.
I do what I'm told.

The guests request *easy on the broth*,
cover their coffee with milk,
their food with hot sauce.
Problem is my hair won't
stay off my face, loose falling

like my dress. It's my appearance
that Paul, the kitchen chief takes
issue with. After all
my bangs do hang, my bra
strap is out of place
and if this, then that
and I'm sorry I'm sorry.

Should have listened to the guest
who warned me not to speak
to the men who work here.
They're mine, she says, *so don't*.

Unremembered

You really don't remember Disney World?
my father asks, *You were eight—*
I must've gotten Goofy's autograph, had
the most fun on *It's a Small World*

ride. Didn't like *Tomorrowland,*
didn't like the wobbling motion of the track.
A place like Frontierland could've made me
happy, I had cowgirl boots. I have a picture

of me on the spinning tea-cups, the rabbit
crying *Rule 42: The queen always wins.*
No, I don't remember any of it.
I don't remember if my mother

sat in the front seat when she should've
sat in the back seat to keep my brother

away from me.

I Had to Pee

and I didn't know I had to.
Was it warmth I gave myself,
soaking the sheets, making
them wet-warm?

Was it bad dreams? When I was
six, my mother showed me how to
wash my sheets in the machine
so she wouldn't have to.

Showed me where the Pine Sol was,
that stench my mattress lived in,
my room lived in.
That was my fragrance.

A Recurring Dream I Had

I was left at the bottom of the hill.
It was kindergarten and so we had taken a field trip.
Kindergarten: there's no number to that grade. I was left
by Miss Anderson, her long blonde hair forgot me.
She always wanted the best for me. Alone
is what's best for me. As always, again,

the next night everyone else got up the hill. Again
I'm left at the bottom of the hill.
I never yelled up, never spoke up the next day about being alone
all night, though night never happened. The next trip
to the bottom of the hill I didn't ask *why* they left me.
No one noticed I'd been left.

In the dream, I kept being left.
Day-after-day, the dream of it happening again,
my parents never looking for me.
One Tuesday night in the third grade, I waited down the hill
for them to come and get me. They couldn't even make the trip
thought they would want me home. I got used to feeling alone

like in real life, that tiny hospital bed, at Children's, me, alone
and two weeks old, every night for a month, left
without a goodnight song, tubes hanging from me, no trip
home, no being held or looked at by my mother's face, my father again
mourned me like I'm dead and buried at the bottom of the hill.
A part of me must have died there, in my parent's minds. The part of me

I still don't know. The me
who is forgotten, ignored, looked over, alone.
The me who couldn't make it, the me who couldn't climb a hill,
couldn't be like Jill of Jack and Jill. I know Jill would have never left
Jack in that nursery rhyme. I'd sing it again
try to whistle it, *to fetch a pail of water*. What a trip

and fall Jack took, maybe he would trip
down my hill someday. Be near me.
But he never did so it's me, again,
only me, feeling so truly alone
that by the two hundredth time I dreamt it I felt meant to be left
and I stayed with that feeling at the bottom of the hill.

I never flew in that dream. Tripped a lot. Rocks, dirt. Left the hill
dream after me dreaming the hill for years. Years waking alone.
Years, again, thinking, *doesn't everyone's life come tumbling after?*

Billiards

It's one game I haven't mastered.
My spin always accidental. I don't break,

the balls go nowhere when I do. I'm best
at winning by default, scratching on

the 8 ball, or, pocketing the 8 before its time.
I like the way a boy plays pool when he's good

at pool. Doesn't have to be cute,
just three shots in a row and know

what he's doing, blowing the chalk off
his stick. Those boys aren't much

for conversation, they're agreeable,
that's all.

Playing Cribbage with My Father

He wants the cribbage board to show off his smarts.
He wins and wins because he's good, I win
because *you're lucky*, he tells me.
You dirtbag! he says, and I couldn't think

of any other way for him to say it or how
not to say it. I cut the deck
and he picks the top card. I can tell he doesn't
like the card when he says *You didn't*

shuffle well enough. And wow those
fifteens add up, my fifteens, the ones
he wishes he had. He punches my shoulder
you scoundrel, you little shit,

and my mother comes in, to yell
a yell I know the neighbors hear.
Don't speak to her that way. My father
doesn't know another way

to speak. This is his intimacy.
This is how I know he loves me.
He hates my pegging style,
I count each hole each time though

I know they're in sets of five.
His double runs are more and more
unfortunate for me.
He's played this game all his life.

Boss's Daughter

I own less than one percent
of the company and have to pay
taxes in so many states
that I have a tax guy. Actually,

I'm tied to my family so much—it's *their* tax guy.
In the wallpaper business it's my job
to write descriptions. I teach folks to see
what they're looking at, I make

florals flowery. I name colors and patterns.
Green isn't green but *fresh water,*
plantain green, highway sign green.
We manufacture too many greens—

like T.S. Eliot says,
Not enough of what I meant, at all. I make
the unremarkable remarkable. The color
Arizona because it's prettier than the color *sand.*

Pinecone I call *country chic.*
The thesaurus is my job's best friend.
I've found thirty-one different ways
to say *manly: gallant, bold, darling,*

dignified, noble, rugged, withstanding.
Paisleys are noble. My brother *withstanding.*
My cousins in the front office I'd categorize as
grasscloth, beige and malingering.

They crunch numbers, manipulate data.
My father's in sales, makes deals and shakes
on them.   My uncle is the CEO, his agenda:
tedious arguments.   He oversees the whole

rolled-up shebang. I write stripes
the size of narrow streets. Even try to name
the office carpet stains: *Abstract Sunsets.*
The office layout I'd name *Maze* or *Labyrinth.*

One Friday while taking inventory
the new warehouse worker appears
at bin location 23, pattern # 148-37524,
the *Wave Lengths* print. His skin

is as beautiful as toile. I'm starving
for a fairytale pinned and wriggling as
I count the rolls of *Cameo Rose*:
One lone rose six inches from the next

lone rose. I know flowers
are the acrobats of wallpaper,
they bunch, trellis, arrange, toss, print, trail.
Never do what true flowers do: Change.

Spare Change

Nothing gold can stay.

—Robert Frost

I'll put change in a stranger's
parking meter if I notice
it's run out of time.
Not only because of the golden
rule, I just can't help
but save someone.

I feed crows dried corn,
watch their yellow beaks
peck at dirt as if
they're making room to pray.

In any orchard I pick
the apples that come off easy.

It's hard to stay gold.
Impossible to stay gold.
The urge to stay is tragic.

The Poem, an Ars Poetica

Poems come to me smelling of trashcan fire
and whiskey. The smell I am to launder
off. And I give each a bed roll. It's my
life. Full-time. I live in this smell. I conjure
this smell, sleep with this smell. I can't
write another sonnet. These poems, homier,
like to camp with a blanket on public cement.
Poems believe in no rules. Ruleless is cozier,
and so the poems stay with me, where they're
not held accountable for making my bed, *being
responsible.* I thought I could write them
asleep in my unmade bed. Every evening
they strike my last match—burnt, sulphury,
needy. I need them to revise the fire in me.

Outreach

Winter finds him on the train station floor
sleeping in the shelter blanket I gave him,
beneath the Alewife sign in bedlam's lower
weather. I bring him socks, toiletries, bring him
a woolen hat. I show up. I always come here
kneel beside him— his shelter, his prayer, his street,
my knees kiss the tiles to face him. Can he hear
the worry in my voice? His eyes are worried
blue. Doesn't he want to live just a little longer?
Most of him seems mostly warm. Midnight, I'm in
the station, it's perfectly dead, no passengers.
He wakes to sleep, and sleeps so I'll wake him.
I'm his moonlight and sun. The stars I spare.
My smokes all smoked. Lost or broken. Or shared.

Taking the Homeless Census

The corner of the laundromat is occupied
by the ex-con with an exhausting past.

He uses missing socks as mittens,
trades socks for cigarettes. Homeless:

sitting-on-a-milk-crate homeless,
facial-hair-unkempt homeless,

publically-collecting-cans homeless,
boozing-at-the-duck-pond homeless,

asking-for-the-time homeless.
Teenagers homeless under bridges

living on benches, or beside the heat vents
in the library, chronic homeless

who find refuge in the holes of
stairwells. The habitually homeless

who have lived four episodes
of homeless in the past two years.

The girl who stocks the shelves
at 7 Eleven tells me she lives

on her friends' couches. The man
I buy a muffin for at Dunkin' Donuts

Sunday mornings goes south
to be homeless in Rhode Island

all winter. In public alleyway
118 three vets have built a room

out of furniture left on the street
by undergraduates. A woman

curled up in a Macy's storefront
leans on the six garbage bags

of her life. On any given night
in January at the Shattuck Shelter

someone will clean up, show up,
ask for a toothbrush, dryness,

five packets of sugar, an outlet.
Sign their name on the sign-in

so that they might be given a bed.
As for the rest of us? Uncounted.

The Poem, Sitting on a Crate

The poem asks me to watch its change
as I walk by. I watch its change.
The poem returns carrying a 7-Eleven
rose wrapped in cellophane for me.

Asks me if I want to see the tent
behind the closed-down movie theatre
where he lives, holds the shower curtain
that is the door open for me as I go in.
I sit in the classroom chair under the tarp
he calls his *tipi*. His floor is the sidewalk
on which he burns the wax bottom

of a candle so the candle can stand. I stand
to go. It's February. I mean, *it's winter.*

The Poem at the Swings

He keeps pushing me, liking
me, both hands pushing my back,

pushing my waist as I hold
the chains singing Edna St. Vincent Millay—

Comes like an idiot,
babbling and strewing flowers

in the voice of Hank Williams.
I hang on, sway the seat, pretend

that I might kick him when
I come back. But I don't.

I'm the only playground
noise, swinging, singing

and he's taking me higher
until my skirt's a flag in the sky.

I've Eaten Spicy

I know which diners have homemade
hot sauce, which have Frank's Red Hot,
which serve Tabasco. dried ghost

peppers make me sweat. I pour red
pepper flakes on anything Italian,
so hot I'm tongue-burned
and my nose gets all runny.
I've scared some people.

I like the bottom of an omelet always
burned. I like things burnt. Toast,
too crispy, home fries overdone,
I like what's hard to cut.

I always have. The fallen cake
that doesn't sit right, coffee grounds
that end up floating
in my cup, wilted greens—
anything out for too long.

The Poem Shows up at My Door

I buzz him in for Cap'n Crunch because
the milk in my fridge is on its last day.

By the end of the bowl we're naked. He counts
the freckles on my back and stops at 54

then we say *freckles* until *freckles*
doesn't mean a thing. Later I'll write his six tattoos.

His teeth leave squirrel prints
across my shoulders, a belt of stars

around my throat.
Should've worn a scarf to write this one.

The Poem in Public

He orders a second drink.
I argue with him until
he promises to sip it slow.
I say, *Let's get some food
in our stomachs.*
The lights go dark in the small
room. And when the first
comic comes on
he mumbles *What a dumbfuck.*
One of his hands tugs
at my skirt like a dog. I pull away.

Three drinks in, he storms
outside into the outside crowd.
I go after him. He
steps off the sidewalk
into the gutter.

Night Is All I've Had of France

A fast pace, a picture
show of two-minute towns

the train doesn't stop for.
All shutters shut. Emptiness

against my open curtain.
Narbonne shows me its legroom,

speaks in whispers
I'm run down! I'm run down!

Toulouse so quick in the quiet—
no time to write my name on

the feeling. This train has a plan,
it's on track, so industrious.

Bolts surrender to beauty.
No postcard to send of this.

Let the train move me
in directions unmediated.

Missing the Poem in Europe

1.

From the bottom of the fire escape,
a man calls up six flights, *Rapunzel,*
Rapunzel, let down your hair.
My hair isn't long enough,
I don't toss down my room key.

The hotel management has called.
Have I seen anyone creeping around
on the fire escape?

2.

Every night I'm in Barcelona
I write what I'm wearing,
how many men looked at
me—I'm a heartbreaker.

Every morning I almost write.
Instead, I count how many
times I can kick a rock
while walking the streets

—ten times, twenty times—
before I lose it to the city.

3.

I'm reading
Of Mice and Men.
'A few miles south
of Soledad. . .' I know
that *soledad* is Spanish for lonely.
But I don't tell the poem that.

Woman Stopped at Customs

Because the pattern on her shirt isn't the Stars
and Stripes she's been purgatoried upon
arrival. Interrogated by Immigration
on how American she is.

Her social media searched through,
I hear her recite each state capital,
name three American desserts—
apple, pecan, Boston cream. Whoopee!

The interrogator reads her passport
for a place of birth, a country she has
to detach from. Maybe she's
been living the dream—

at a nail salon, the life Horatio Alger wrote about.
The interrogator says she's *Muslim.* America
is where she's being terrorized. Home
is where she was civil-warred.

Home

I mean, shouldn't someone be back home
at the end of the day? Where people go is home.

Home should be a place to stay.
The corner calls the street home.

Home for cowboys is campfire.
For weather— sky's home.

Frost calls *the place where, when you have*
to go there, they have to take you in, home.

For the circus it's Big Top. For fruit, rind's home.
Sweaters call the cedar trunk home.

Tell myself *Come home,*
Alexis. And so, I head home.

Dream on the 17th Floor

I'm watering my flower box
when the woman in the apartment
across the way leans her head
out her window to tell me

boiled pasta with marinara
ended up being their last supper.
He finished first, walked out to the fire
escape and over, as she sat finishing
her pasta, sopping her bread in the sauce.

I want to reach out, touch her hand.
I don't.

I notice a mourning dove,
semi-hobbling on her rail,
hanging around, accumulating fame.

She shows me the crack of her
eave where he's nesting.

Goodnight Is Never Goodnight

I wake crying for the things
I've already cried for,
wanting to forget how bad
dreams go out to dinner,
a candlelit place

where my lover tells the waitress
her eyes are more than blue.
He tells her she's as smooth as sea glass,
as soft as all the petals of a rose.

Unsurprising never stops surprising.
Damp sheets, and my pillow's
on the floor. In every nightmare
someone dies or someone dies
after being dead already
and I'm O, so tired of sleep
without rest.

The Pin-up Girl I Want to Be

is a poster hanging in my closet, is all *oops,*
my top is falling off, holding a rose,

pink, practically with her fingertips, petals
babying her nose. Even I can smell that arousal

as she embraces her right breast. Chin up,
she's revving for a downtown night.

Her other hand plays
with the telephone cord, tempting with moves

unmoved. Is she answering that call
or hanging up? I can choose any

misconception I want. She's
on her back, one knee bent and the other

crossed over, high-heel dangling.
She's pinned here, all satin in

a classy-broad way. Poised in forever,
forever.

Radical Surgery

Let me show you the scar
waist-deep down my chest.

Deep enough to deserve
a get well card.

I was just being born—
to be cut open and stitched

the way a sparrow knots
its beak in sandwich crust.

My body turning blue
like it was winter at the beginning

of July. Still I dress for weather,
and any Sylvia-Plath sky— *the moon*

has nothing to be sad about.
I rely on that moon, my courage as deep-

wooded as a star's. If I point to my heart
like my hand's a gun would you love me?

Reading about Death Row in *The Times*

The people they murdered didn't ask for a last meal.
—a state lawmaker

The guy who murdered his daughter wanted
an olive, just one olive with the pit still in it.
The triple homicide wanted a pound
of strawberries, a king-size Milky Way,

one more Take 5, Mary Jane's. The cop
killer wanted sugarless pie. Most wanted
breakfast like they were starting their day.
Took their eggs beaten or scrambled,

over-easy, sunny-side-up and cage-
free, their steak prepared rare. The vet
who blew up a post office in Abilene
wanted a dish of ice cream, melted.

Charlie who spent thirty years on Death
Row wanted a pizza to be given to a homeless
person on his behalf. As for the man who
wanted to eat a plate of dirt, REQUEST DENIED.

The Poem as Metaphor

I bring home a hermit crab
in his shell from Cape Cod. Set him
up in a fat glass jar with other shells
he can move into. Serve him cut kale.

I figure he's having the time of his life,
feeling nothing of October
in my bathroom with the heat cranked.

I tack a map of his island
behind his jar. Name him *Wellfleet*
so he won't be homesick.
It's my say-so, my playing God.
I'm the gull he hides from.

I give him saltwater which
only makes him scratch
at air. I try to sit him on dirt
from my tomato plant
but it doesn't work.

I suppose he needs
the island I took from him.

Scratch-off Ticket

In the vacant lot near my place all the cats
are stray, their bones all looking
the sad-same, like rodents in a darker way.

No one feeds them. No child allowed
to hunch down and play. I hunch down.
I root for the underdog. Every day

I buy a ticket, the scratch-off kind. Scratch it off
with a penny. I don't use the penny
from the dish at the register.

Every ticket needs its own penny. If I find
a penny on the sidewalk, and use it to win
I keep that penny for the next game.

If I lose, that penny's out. Each ticket is always
the grocer's choice, I make Albert decide.
I blame him every time I lose.

I tear the ticket to pieces. Litter
the vacant lot with shred.
I don't hold onto bad luck.

Allegiance in Five Stanzas

I will write the rest of my life
how steadfast I am.
It's my job,
it's all I can do.

How steadfast, I am
a carriage horse,
it's all I can do,
my boots clip-clop the pavement.

A carriage horse
breaking my heart on the page,
my boots clip-clop the pavement,
I carry everyone along.

I break my heart on the page,
writing my bridled life,
I carry everyone along.
Born for this and to this.

Writing my bridled life
is my job.
Born for this and to this
I will write the rest of my life.

After Breaking up with the Poem

I binge watch *Melrose Place*. I've been through
a lot in this show: eight Thanksgivings here,
Four trips to Mexico, nineteen weddings,
twenty-three divorces, six arrests, thirty-five
court dates, twelve broken windows,

No eating disorder storylines but plenty
of suicide, plenty of secret pasts
and false-alarm pregnancies.
Nobody ever leaves
LA, no one gets away.

I can't even get away—
that's why I watch. I almost
don't pick up when a friend
from college calls to ask me
to loan her seven hundred

dollars to pay for an abortion.
I'll say yes. It'll feel good
to help her not have a baby.
On *Melrose Place* the dead show up
three seasons after they die.

When Someone Asks Me Where I Go

to school I never want to
say *Harvard. Harvard* always
seems like a name drop.
What I like about *Harvard*

Extension is the part-time nighttime feel,
students fresh from off the job.

In Wednesday night Logic, every notebook is
open for the math of words,
syllogisms. The professor keeps using

the example *All poets are morons.*
He chalks the words on the board.
Instead I write
in my notebook—

All professors are morons.
Therefore, the students
in my class are morons.

The professor argues that logic
is not about nouns, it's about
argument. And I know all arguments
have to come to an end.

I am a poet because I know how to break
a line—

That's an argument.
Reason is a premise.
It supports a conclusion:
Poetry is not logical. Metaphor is
not logical either—My umbrella, for example
knows for sure that it's raining.

On the #86 Bus to Harvard Graduation
Class of 2015

I'd thought about wearing my tasseled cap
but it clashed with my bus persona
so I carried it in my bookbag. Commencement
was at the Drama Center where I saw *Prometheus*

Bound: by Zeus in chains. I'm still
that story my mother tells:
At two I refused to wear the flowered dress.
Even now I wouldn't think twice about stealing

fire from the gods. Kicked out of every
school I went to, asking for trouble all the time.
Sure, I'm proud to be a Harvard graduate.
Still, I can't believe this robe is mine.

On Every Tree at the Reservoir

there's a missing boy poster.
Had he gone for a swim too cold?

Fallen in? Wanted to see city lights
bounce off the water?

On every tree his flannel shirt
plaid and nondescript.

What keeps me is how much
I don't know him,

how much he's become
known for being MISSING.

I mean, he disappeared on this path
like a magician's hat disappears.

I walk the reservoir, where they search
for him— don't give up

until he's found there.
For me, he stays

on the bottom even after
he's floated up.

Having a Second Cup

I like the aimless comforts,
the streetlamps that flutter on
before night is night.

The waiter calls me *Dollface*,
Dollface makes my cheeks rosy,
my eyebrows perfectly shaped.

I'm reading *The Dead*—
Better pass boldly into that other world
and James Joyce is

interrupted by teenage girls at the next table
buzzing—how lucky they are, how no one
in their families has died. They pour

laughable amounts of sugar
into coffee cups, stir the spoon
as loud as church bells.

If James Joyce had said
starlings weren't starlings
but grackles I'd believe him.

Map of Boston, 2013

From my fire escape a blue balloon
has strayed from its party, caught on a tree.
It's out of breath, tired of the bullying wind.
From up here I can make out
the other side of the playground.
and a dandelion in the alley
grows out of a crack. I didn't grow

up well mannered, no linen napkins
on my lap, but paper plates on Centre
Street, one of childhood's main drags.
I've moved out of my folks' house
where the one leaf in my salad
was iceberg. Learned to lose

my mother's Boston accent, learned how
dirty half-melted snow can get.
I could show you certain corners of Mattapan
clotheslines keep high-rises
from falling. Fights break out,
windows stay broken, hate crimes
caked in paint on storefronts—
Even I was dangerous
once, buying late summer smack,
overheating the car on Blue Hill Ave.

These days, it's murder on Boylston
Street, it's pressure cookers tearing
the Marathon apart, blowing legs
loose, like bricks in the blizzard
of '96. The Commonwealth is constantly
in revision. Even I edit myself,
take out every *never*, each *always*:
I used to think explosions
near the finish line meant Victory.

I Tell the Janitor I'm Moving Out

and he says *pobre chica*.
He's right, I like this place:
three years on my own with a view

of the reservoir, the train waking
me and the sun waking me,
I could be naked and no would notice.

I'll miss the do-it-yourself elevator.
End of the hall, my door. I added a lock
to that door. Made myself safe.

My landlady is selling, and I'm not
buying, is how it happened.
I'll move to a place with more windows.

But mostly I loved these windows,
I'd sit on the sill or else lean on the radiator,
smoking five thousand thousand cigarettes.

No car of mine parked in *Resident
Parking*. The fire escape is where I'd watch
the unseeable city stars.

In the kitchen, I loved using
the built-in clothesline and the pull-out
ironing board that made me start

ironing blouses. I have more jars
than silverware, always a bag
of coffee beans to grind.

Elegy

i.m. m.b.s. 1972-2014

Autumn is the season of slow reside,
shredding ivy, green-turned-brown.
Leaves absolve the earth before they die.

Leaves well kept, blown, layering the sky,
stepped on, so settled in sky-sound—
autumn is the season of slow reside.

Sun shows late for the fallen. Shines
stubborn, a street lamp in that polis of clouds.
Leaves absolve the earth before they die.

Leaves stripped and torn as they pine
for frost, first-snow, blood on the ground,
autumn is the season of slow reside.

Leaf-smoke catches in the eye, the kind
of worldly pain all birches bear. How
leaves absolve the earth! After they die

the sky will weather and rain less light.
December will also die. How round
autumn is, the season of slow reside.
Leaves absolve the earth before they die.

Also by Alexis Ivy:

Romance with Small–Time Crooks
BlazeVOX [books], 2013

Taking the Homeless Census is printed in Adobe Caslon Pro.

www.saturnaliabooks.org